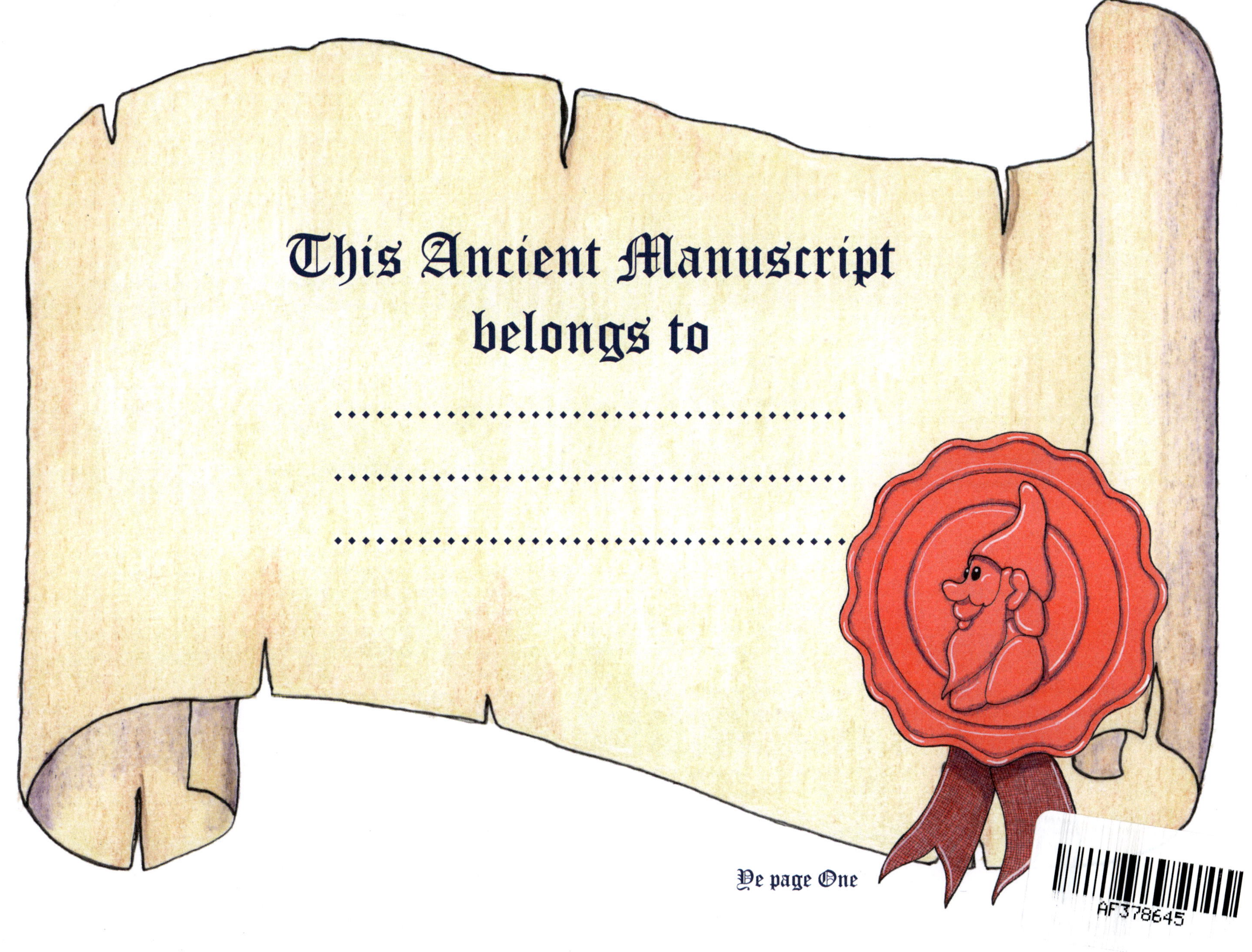

This Ancient Manuscript
belongs to

Ye page One

## Published by...

Bonadventure Chronicles The Quest Volume 2
First published in Great Britain in 2018
Armcher Productions

ISBN 978-1-905672-40-0
Copyright © Armand Foster 2017



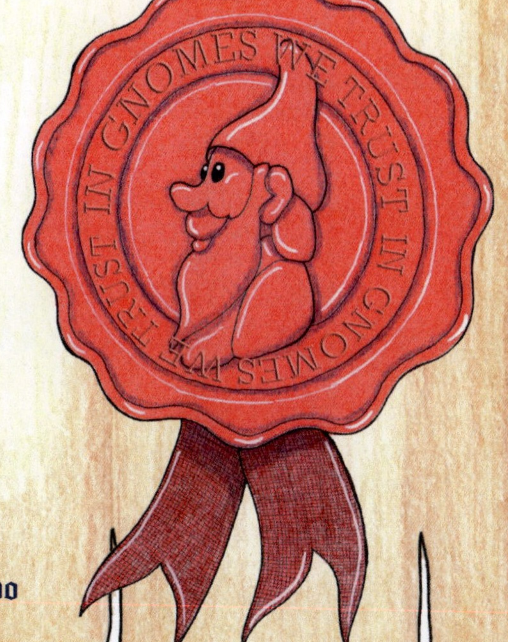


Ye page Two

What Ho Fellow Explorers.
Back in the mists of time,
Bonadventure Vanmolle, the great
Belgian Explorer, Cad, Bounder and
all round Bad Egg mounted
an Expedition to the Amazon
to find the lost Treasure mislaid
by the Spanish Conquistadors.
To do this he travelled up the
Amazon on a series of inflatable
mattresses, for comfort you'll
understand.
Amazingly the fearless bounder
suffered a disaster, someone pricked
his mattresses and he sunk
without trace for ten minutes
in the Amazon.
What luck, while underwater
he found the lost treasure
in an old rotting suitcase!
Once again he hid his Booty
on the beautiful Isle of Alba.

Armand Foster, his Great
Grandson the Arty Explorer
is once again on the case.
He travels the beautiful
land painting scenes and
searching endlessly for the illicit
booty hidden by the dastardly
Bonadventure. Help him by
finding the hidden treasure.
Don't forget to find him, his Dog Oz
and the wily Meerkat Musprat who
travel with him. Good luck!

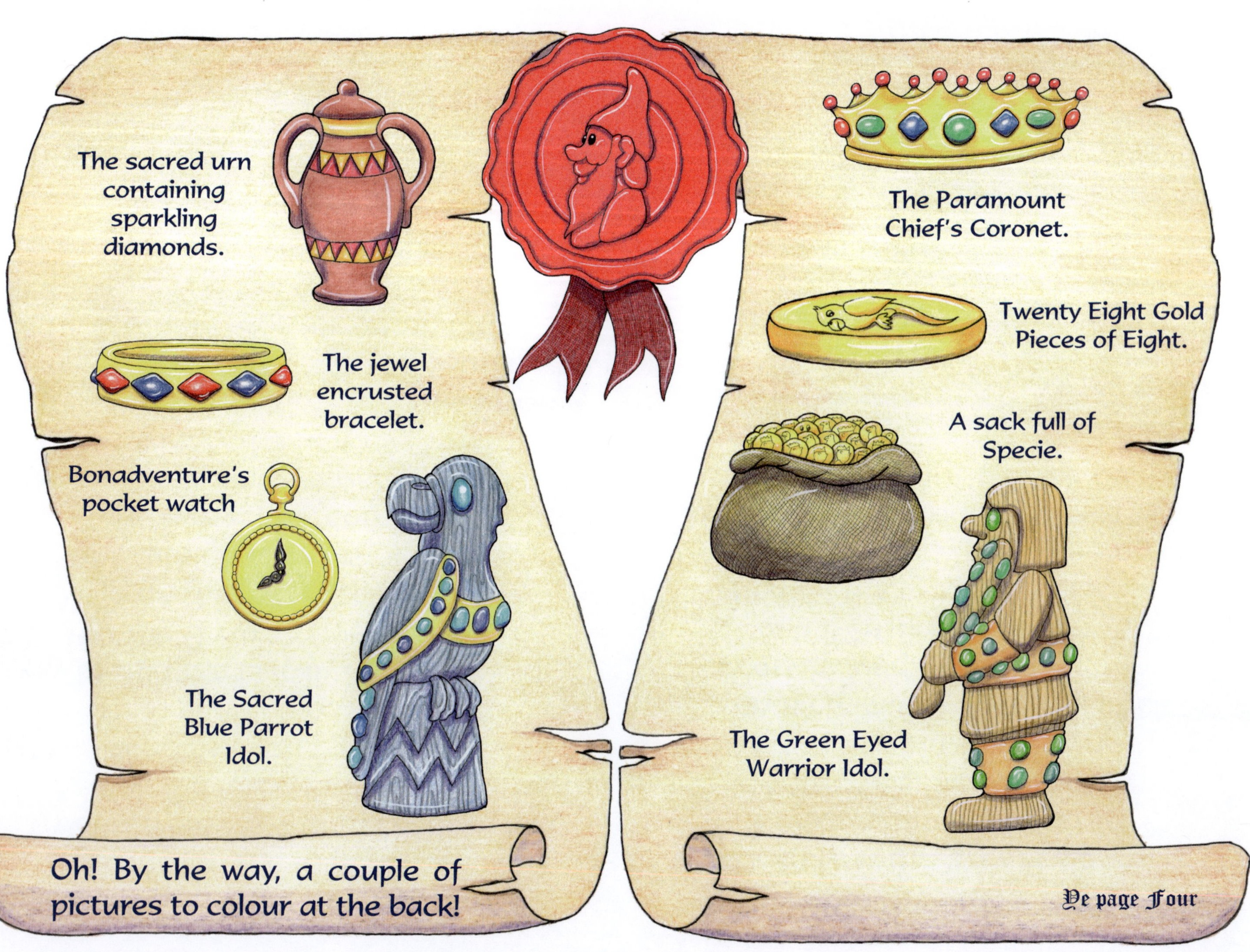

The sacred urn containing sparkling diamonds.
The jewel encrusted bracelet.
Bonadventure's pocket watch
The Sacred Blue Parrot Idol.
The Paramount Chief's Coronet.
Twenty Eight Gold Pieces of Eight.
A sack full of Specie.
The Green Eyed Warrior Idol.
Oh! By the way, a couple of pictures to colour at the back!
Ye page Four

Remember Dear Questors,
that in all the scenes there
are many unusual Characters
for you to find:
The Menneken Pis,
The Parrots and Parakeets.
The Tortoise and the Hare,
The Wily Fox.
Bats, Vultures, and not
to forget the Gnomes.
All to be found,
identified and
included in your Census.
Have fun!

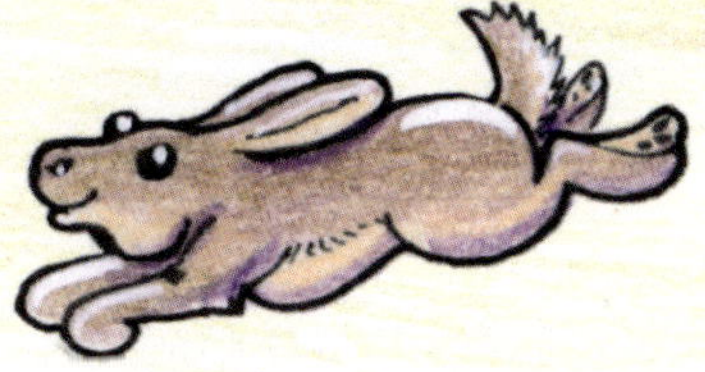

You will also find
small blank seals
like this for you
to place your
cipher or mark
when the object
is found.

# The Great Seal

Can you see that there
is a letter embossed
onto the Great Seal
of the House of Bonadventure
Hidden in the scenes
are twelve such seals, your
quest is to find them
and the hidden word.

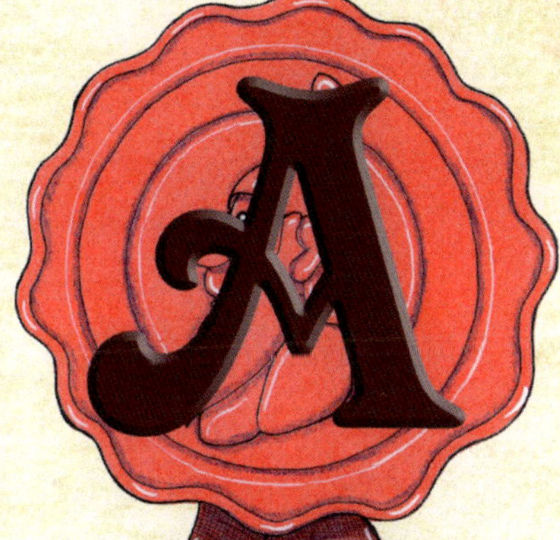

Good luck explorers!

Apart from the beautiful scenes from the Isle of Alba
there are ancient scrolls bearing puzzles  in
this Manuscript for you to decipher.

How many of the following can you find in the scenes in this ancient scroll?

Horses

Pigs

Elephants (What is the big difference between African and Asian Elephants?)

How many Burglars (Is this a Crime wave?)

How many Policemen or Bobbies, Don't forget two Sheriffs?

Search all the Scenes
and find......
A Gorilla
A Chimpanzee
A Giraffe
and Five Foxes

There is one Scene that
is certainly not on
the Isle of Alba, or
is it, Could it be
in the Wild West of
the beautiful Island?
What do you think?

Each scene has a title like the one below.
Can you think of a better or funnier one?

## Search the town square for...

A man with a clip board.

Vikings.

A dangerous Butcher.

A Catapult.

Stocks.

A Pawnbrokers sign.

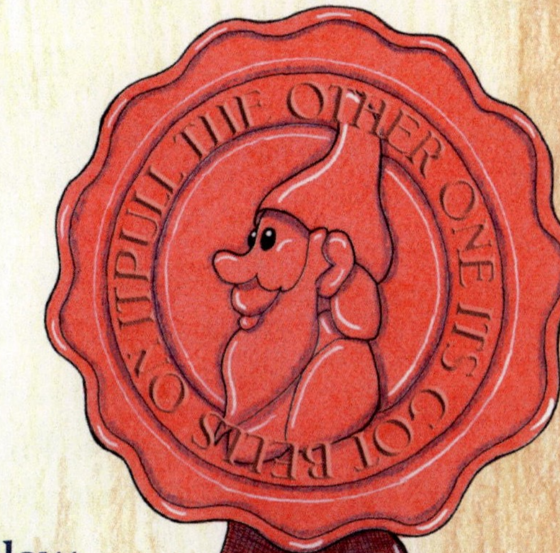


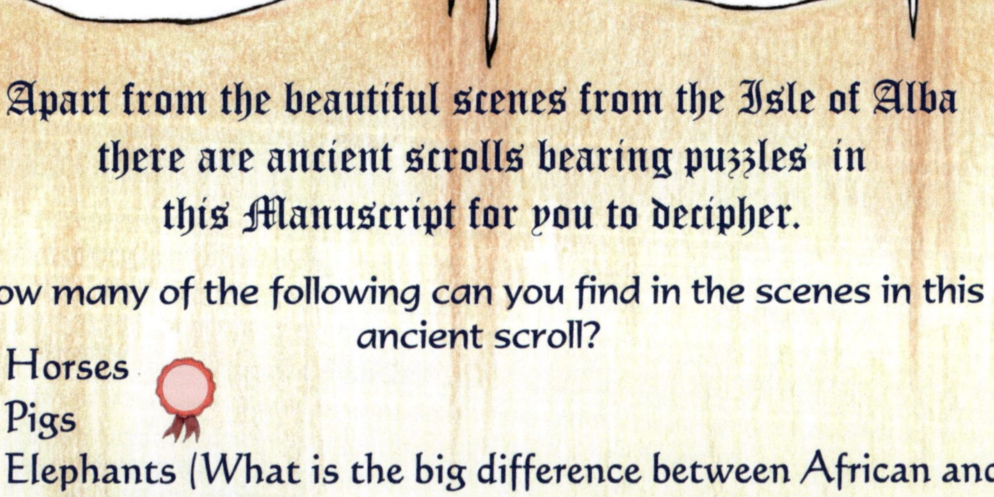

## The day the Fox came to town.

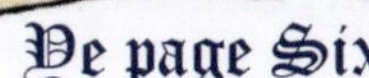

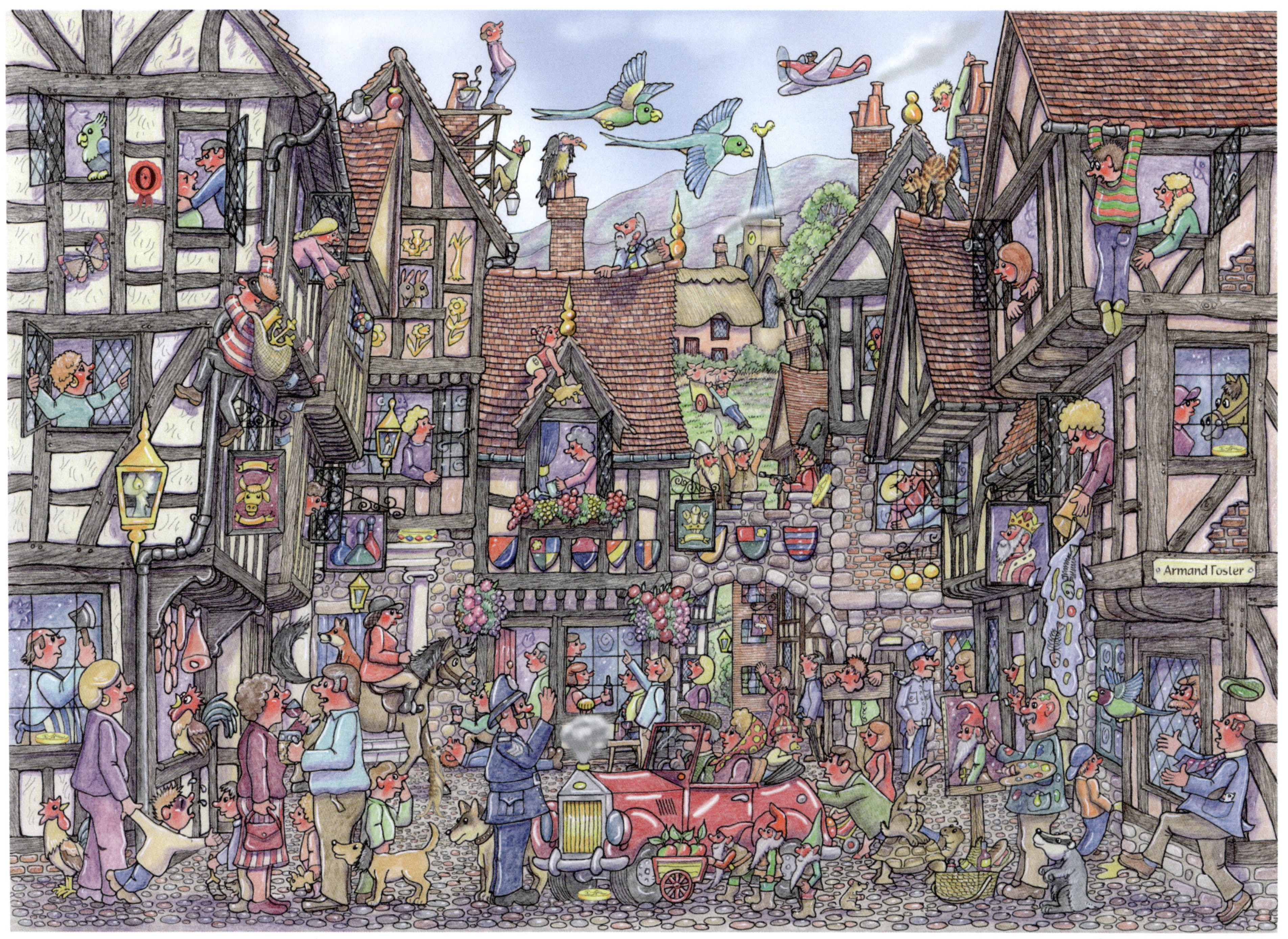


Ye page Seven

Golly and thrice gosh!
An ancient shield bearing
a secret message, or something!

TIMBERDFJIB
HSIFTIOPSTE
AMOGHBREEZE
TOATMNWGQUR
CARAVANUFPT
HUSOAWEQUAY
TWOBNSDUNWA
PAXLEGEDNIC
OVCIOHCFEQH
AENDUCKOLFT

Can you find the 21 hidden
Words, Questors?

Find the following in ye seaside cove;

An angry Captain
A bearded Captain
A crate of Chickens
A Chicken in a basket
A crate of Pigs
Two Bats
Two Ducks
Two Flying Fish
Two Dolphins
Two Crabs
Five Sea Gulls
Two Jackdaws
A Wise Owl
Two Vultures
A Caravan
A Flipper
A second Horse
A man in the attic
An orange Cobra
A frightened Surfer

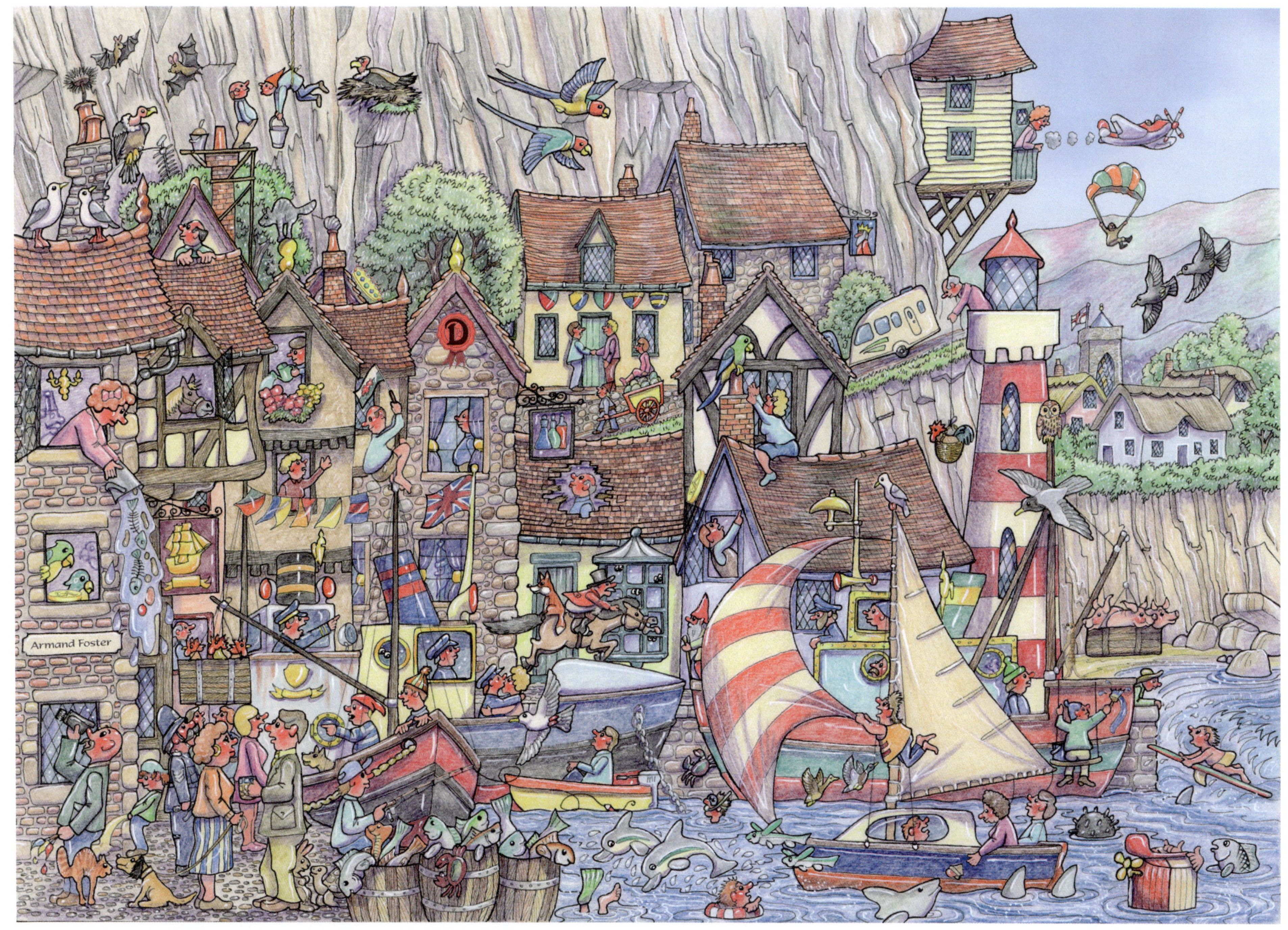


Ye page Nine

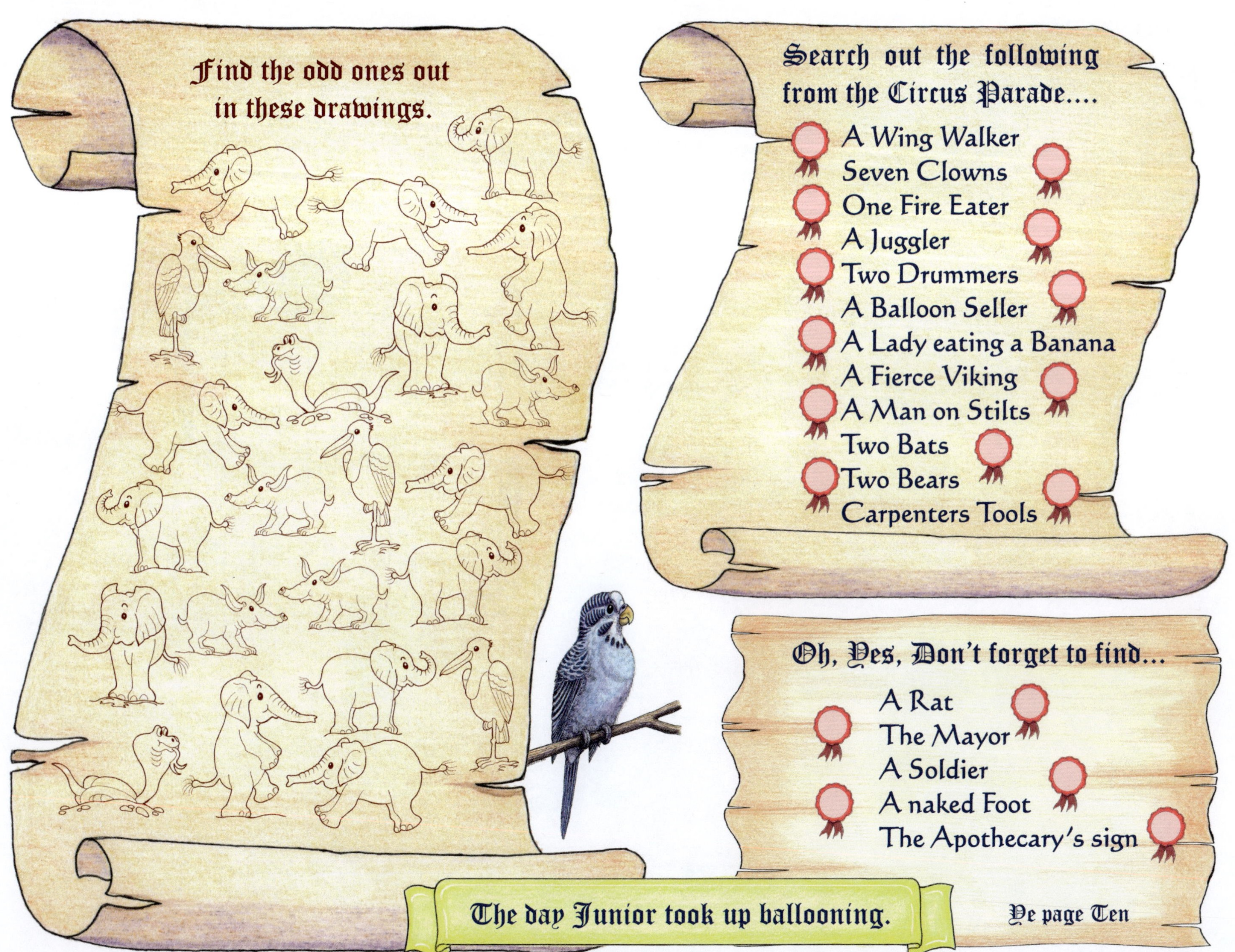
Find the odd ones out
in these drawings.

Search out the following
from the Circus Parade....

A Wing Walker
Seven Clowns
One Fire Eater
A Juggler
Two Drummers
A Balloon Seller
A Lady eating a Banana
A Fierce Viking
A Man on Stilts
Two Bats
Two Bears
Carpenters Tools

Oh, Yes, Don't forget to find...

A Rat
The Mayor
A Soldier
A naked Foot
The Apothecary's sign

The day Junior took up ballooning.

Ye page Ten

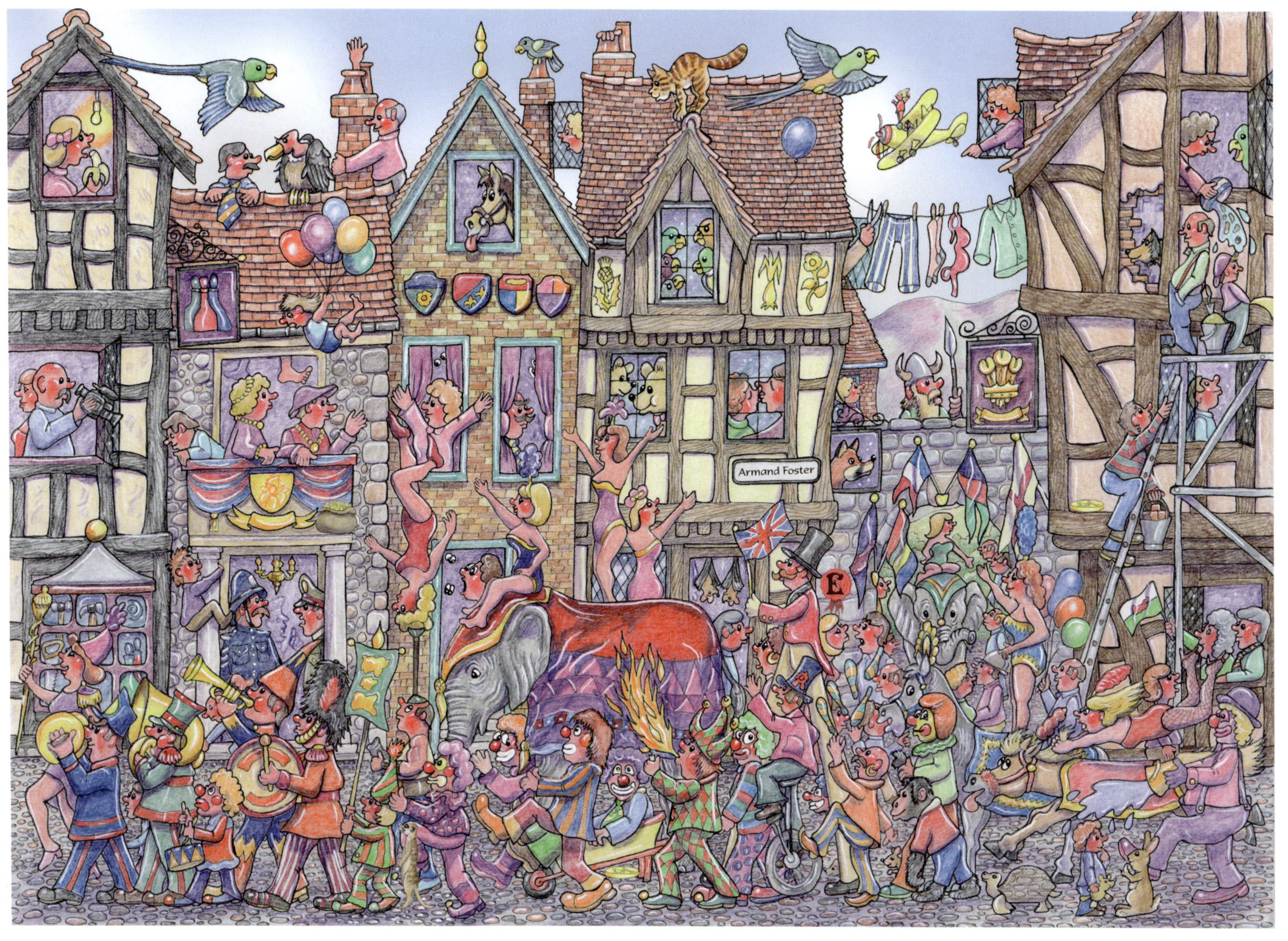

Ye page Eleven

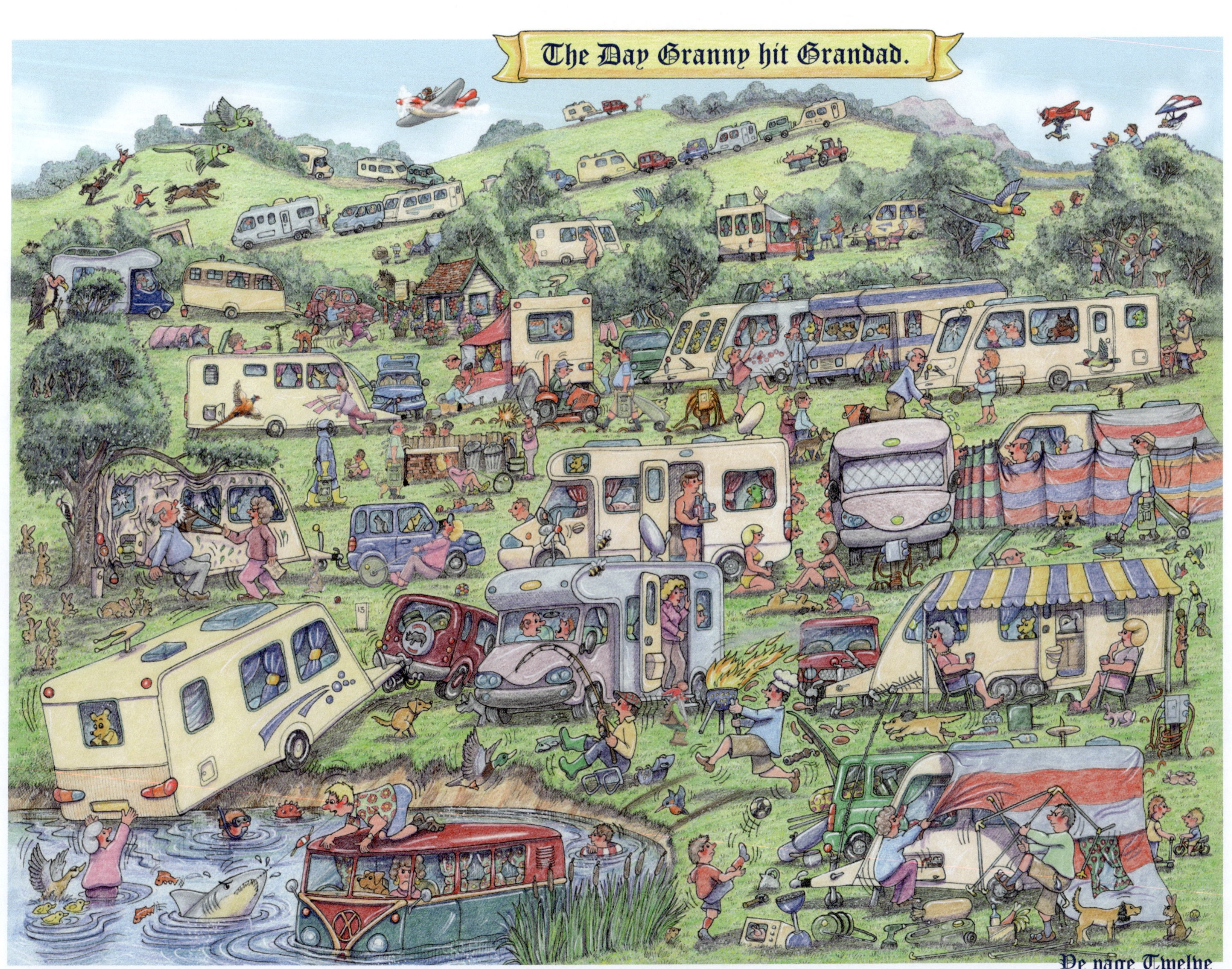
The Day Granny hit Grandad.

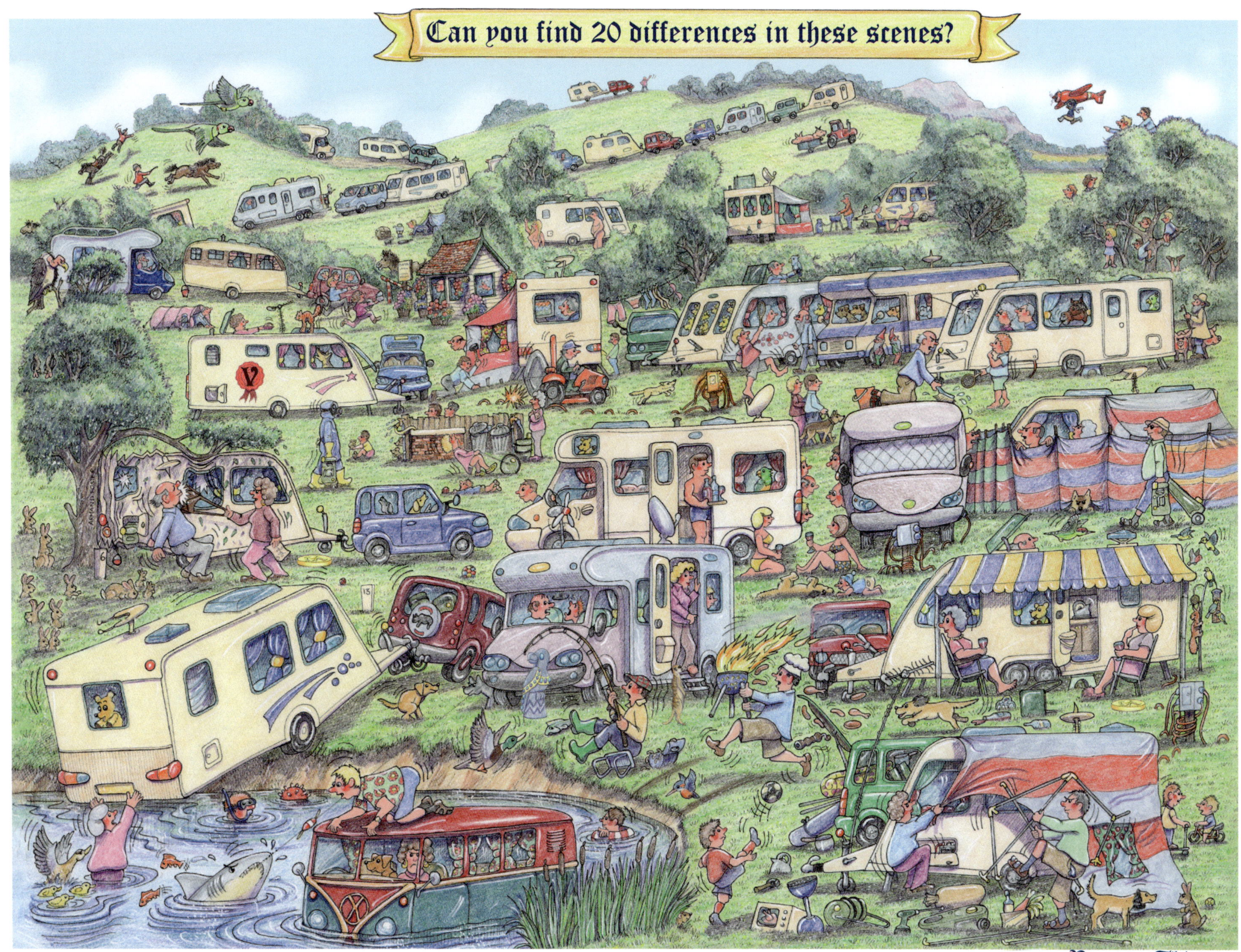

Can you find 20 differences in these scenes?
Ye page Thirteen

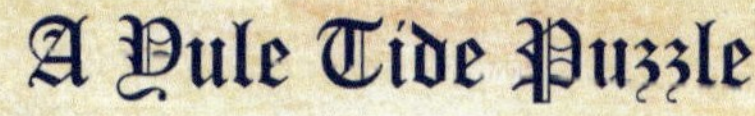

**Find the hidden word**

## ACROSS
2. Hymns sung at Yuletide.
5. See 2 down.
6. Santa has lots to give out.
7. She's clinging onto 5 across.
8. Traditionally hung on front door.

## DOWN
1. It goes with Ivy.
2&5. A decorated fir.
3. They have music sheets to help.
4. Another name for a lamp.

# How many Santas

How many Santas can you find in this scene?

How many beautifully wrapped presents can you find?

How many Teddy Bears are there?

How many Reindeer are there?

**The day Rudolf rebelled!**

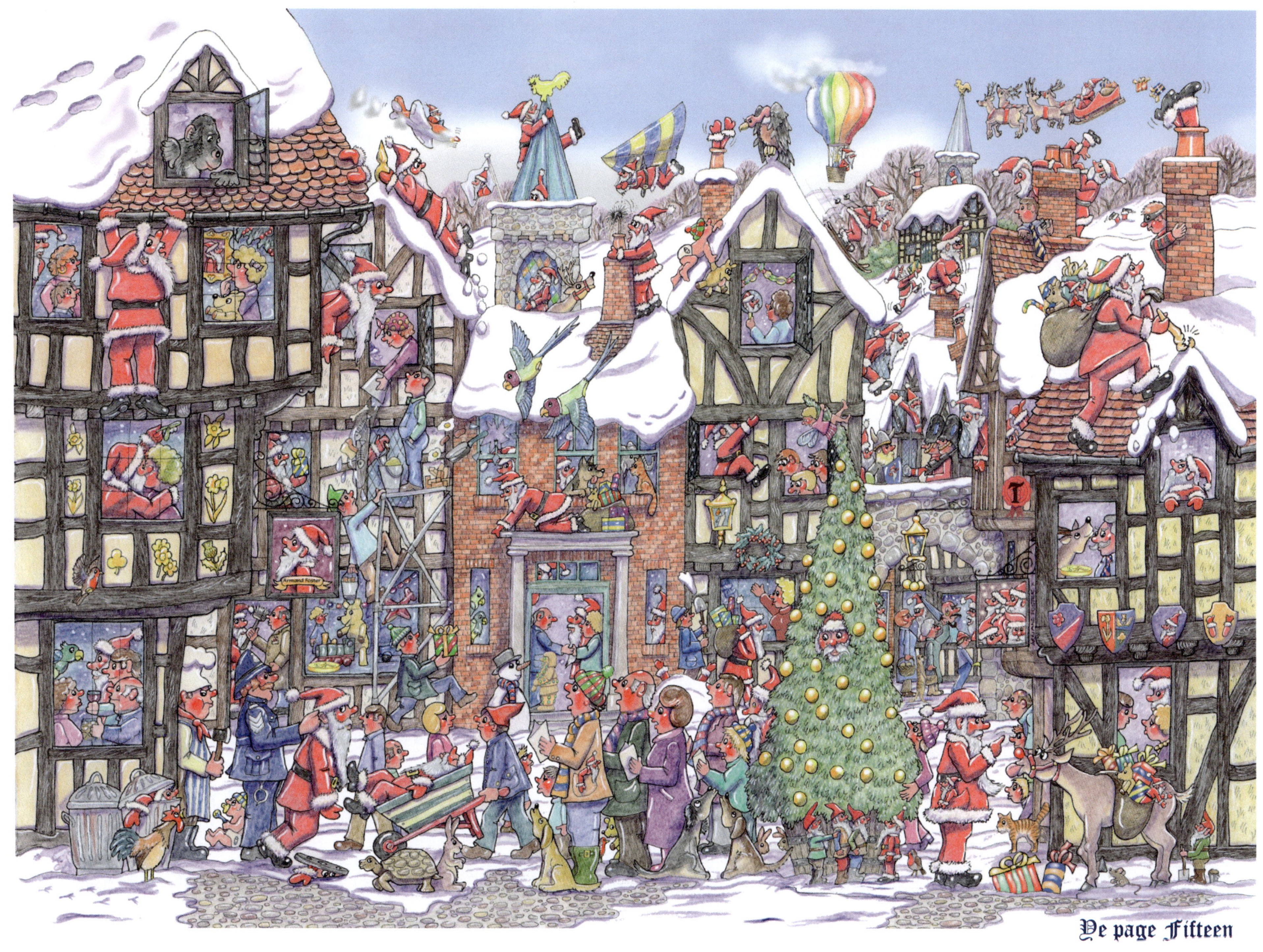

Ye page Fifteen

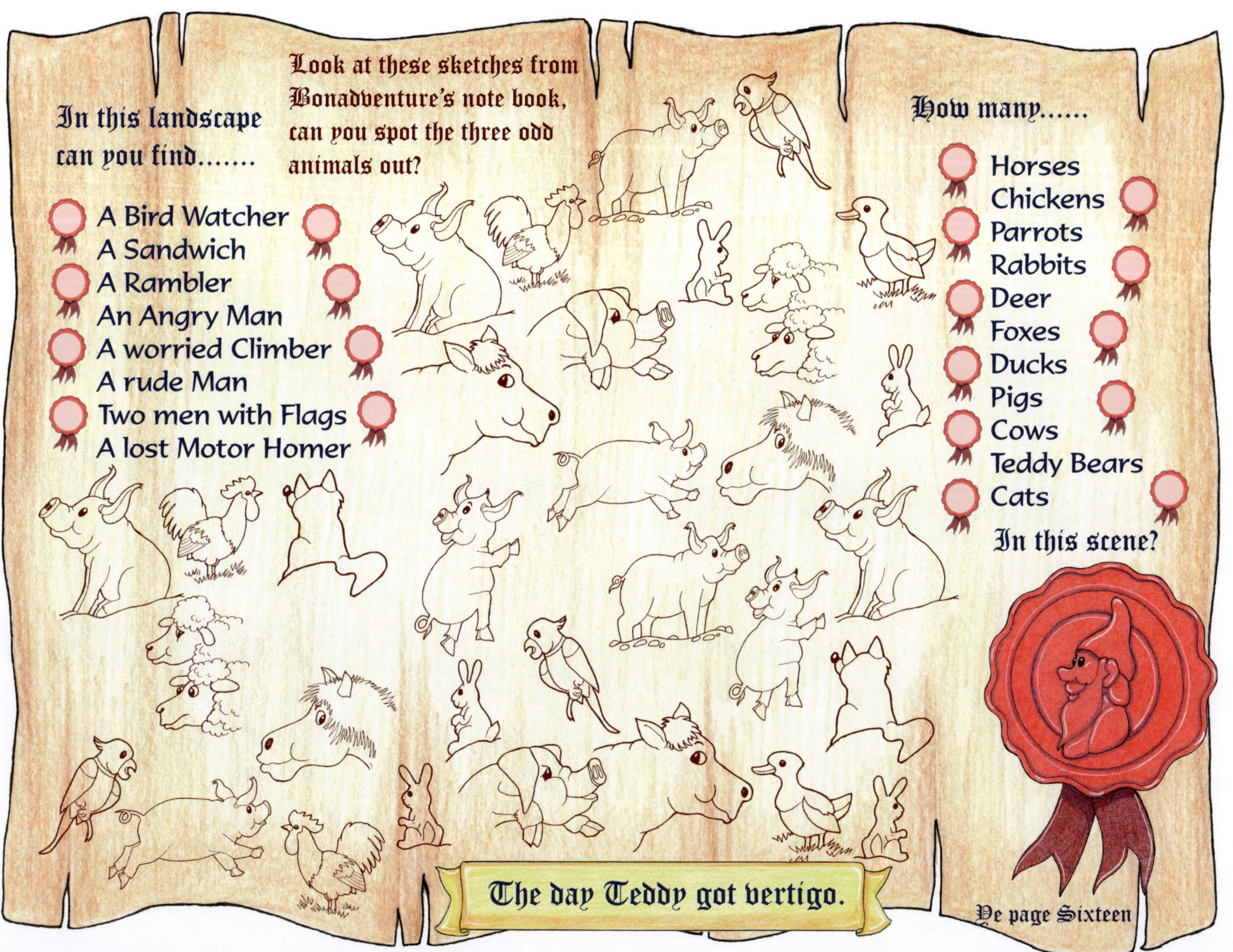
In this landscape
can you find.......

A Bird Watcher
A Sandwich
A Rambler
An Angry Man
A worried Climber
A rude Man
Two men with Flags
A lost Motor Homer

Look at these sketches from
Bonadventure's note book,
can you spot the three odd
animals out?

How many......

Horses
Chickens
Parrots
Rabbits
Deer
Foxes
Ducks
Pigs
Cows
Teddy Bears
Cats

In this scene?

The day Teddy got vertigo.

Ye page Sixteen

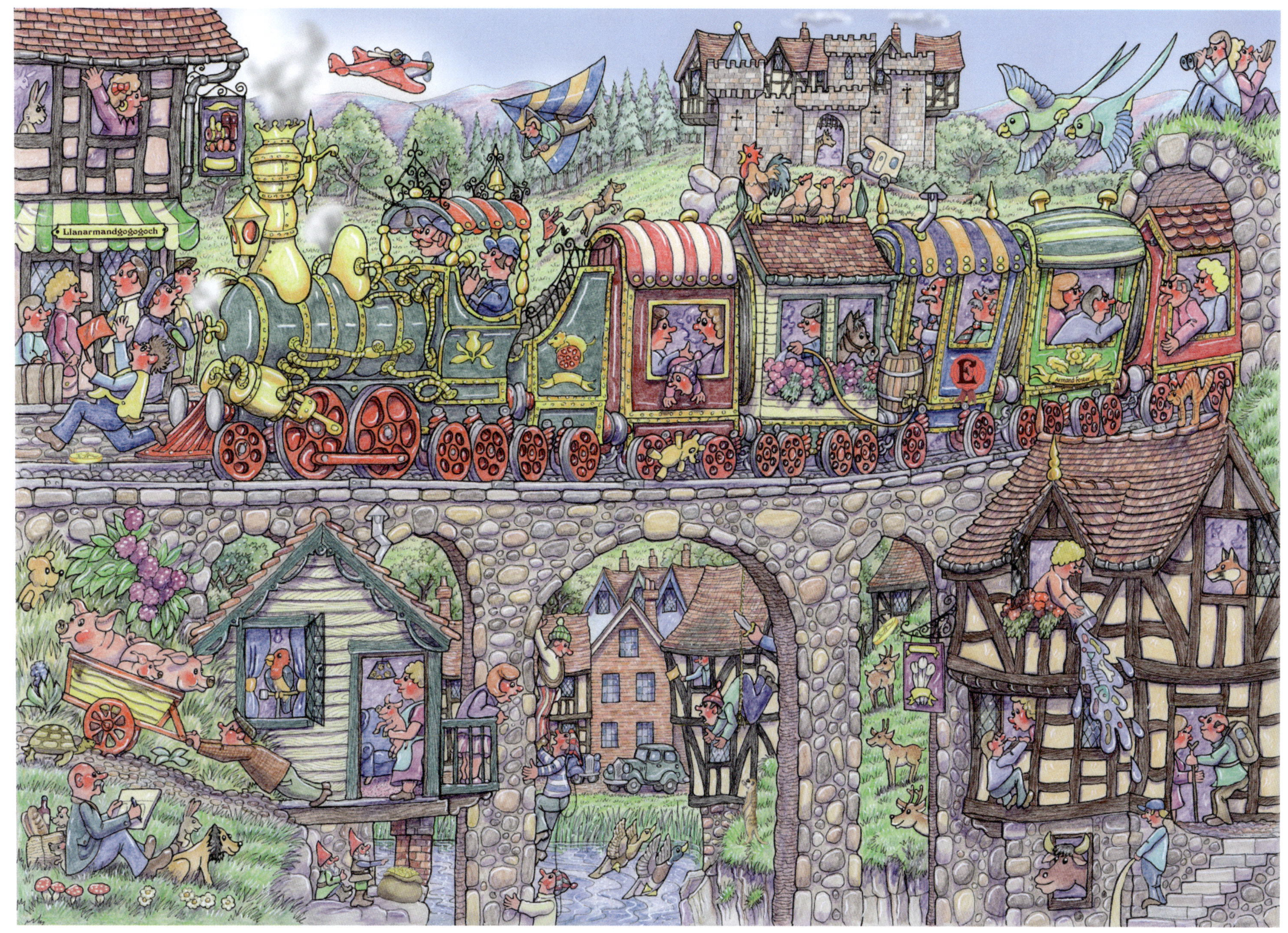

Llanarmandgogogoch

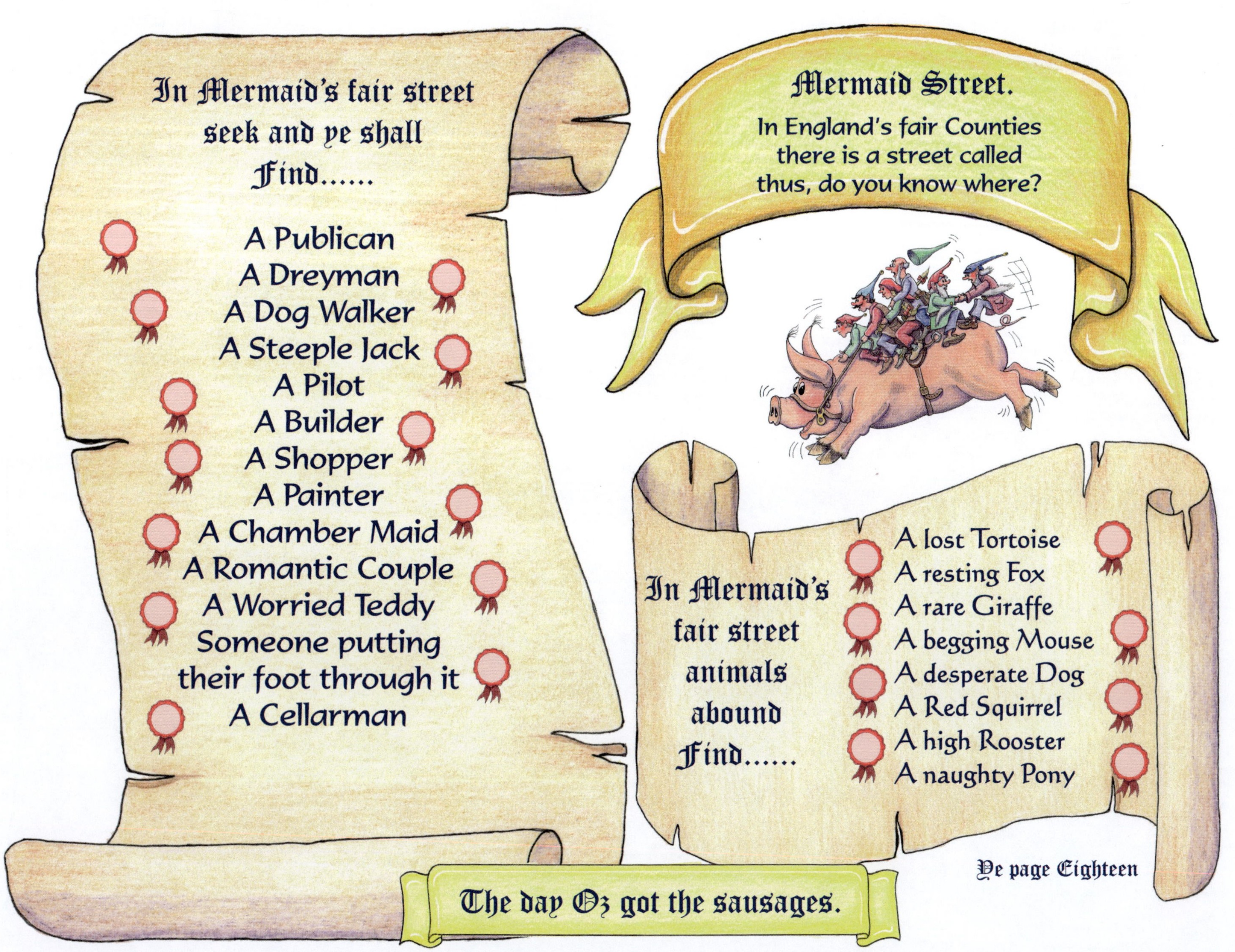

In Mermaid's fair street
seek and ye shall
Find......

A Publican
A Dreyman
A Dog Walker
A Steeple Jack
A Pilot
A Builder
A Shopper
A Painter
A Chamber Maid
A Romantic Couple
A Worried Teddy
Someone putting
their foot through it
A Cellarman

Mermaid Street.

In England's fair Counties
there is a street called
thus, do you know where?

In Mermaid's
fair street
animals
abound
Find......

A lost Tortoise
A resting Fox
A rare Giraffe
A begging Mouse
A desperate Dog
A Red Squirrel
A high Rooster
A naughty Pony



The day Oz got the sausages.

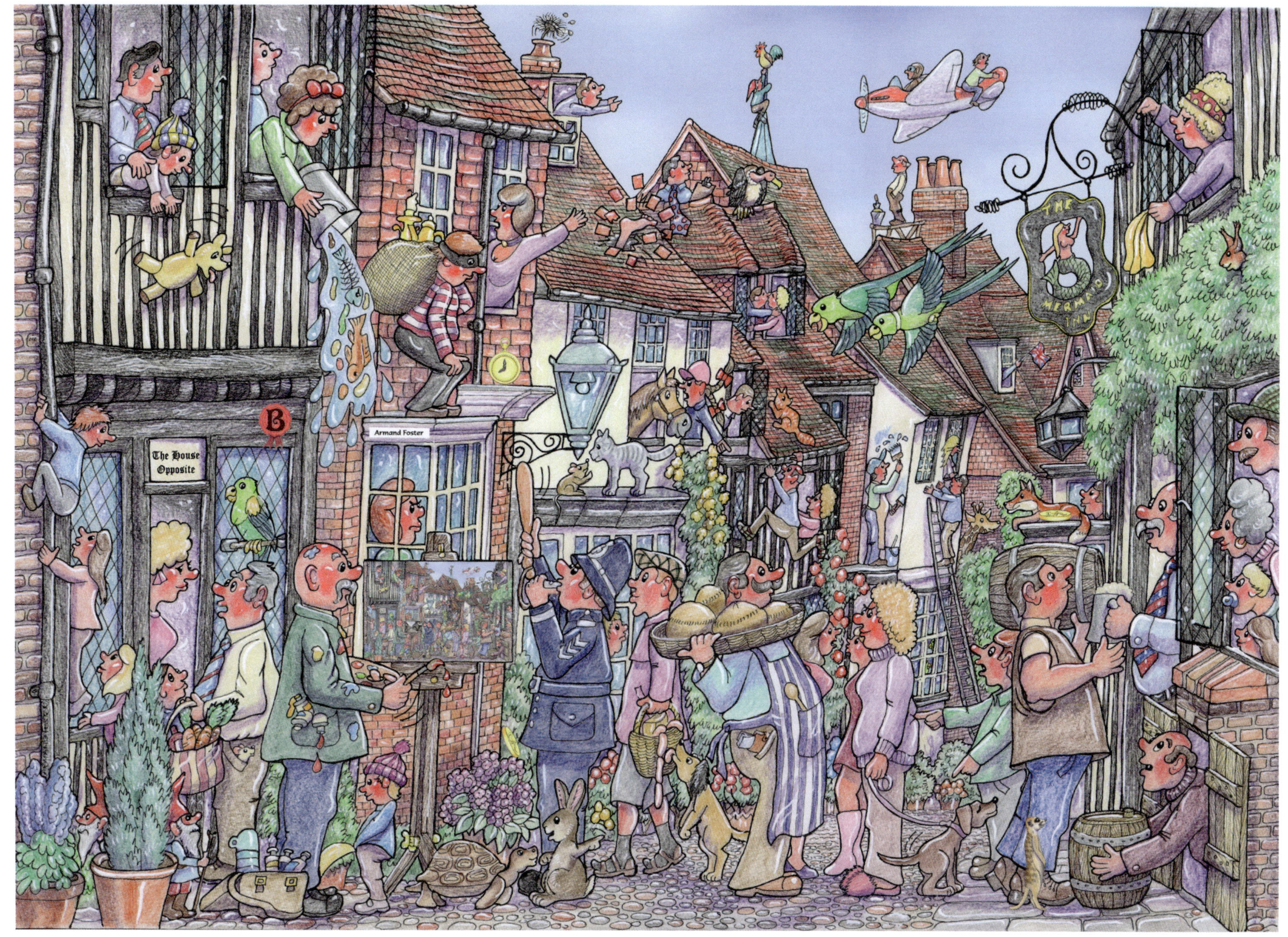


Ye page Nineteen

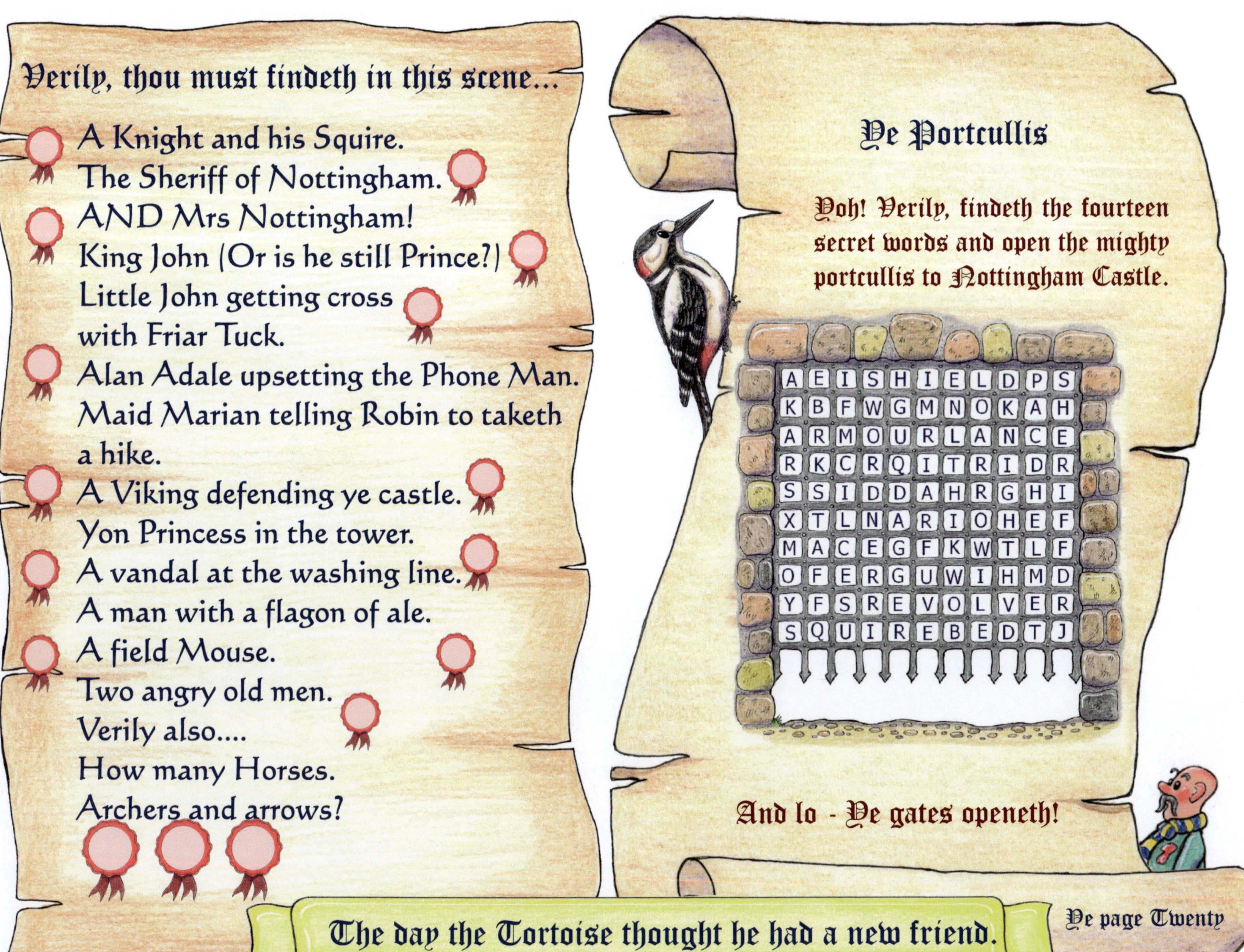

Verily, thou must findeth in this scene...

A Knight and his Squire.
The Sheriff of Nottingham.
AND Mrs Nottingham!
King John (Or is he still Prince?)
Little John getting cross
with Friar Tuck.
Alan Adale upsetting the Phone Man.
Maid Marian telling Robin to taketh
a hike.
A Viking defending ye castle.
Yon Princess in the tower.
A vandal at the washing line.
A man with a flagon of ale.
A field Mouse.
Two angry old men.
Verily also....
How many Horses.
Archers and arrows?

Ye Portcullis

Yoh! Verily, findeth the fourteen
secret words and open the mighty
portcullis to Nottingham Castle.

A E I S H I E L D P S
K B F W G M N O K A H
A R M O U R L A N C E
R K C R Q I T R I D R
S S I D D A H R G H I
X T L N A R I O H E F
M A C E G F K W T L F
O F E R G U W I H M D
Y F S R E V O L V E R
S Q U I R E B E D T J

And lo - Ye gates openeth!

The day the Tortoise thought he had a new friend.

Ye page Twenty

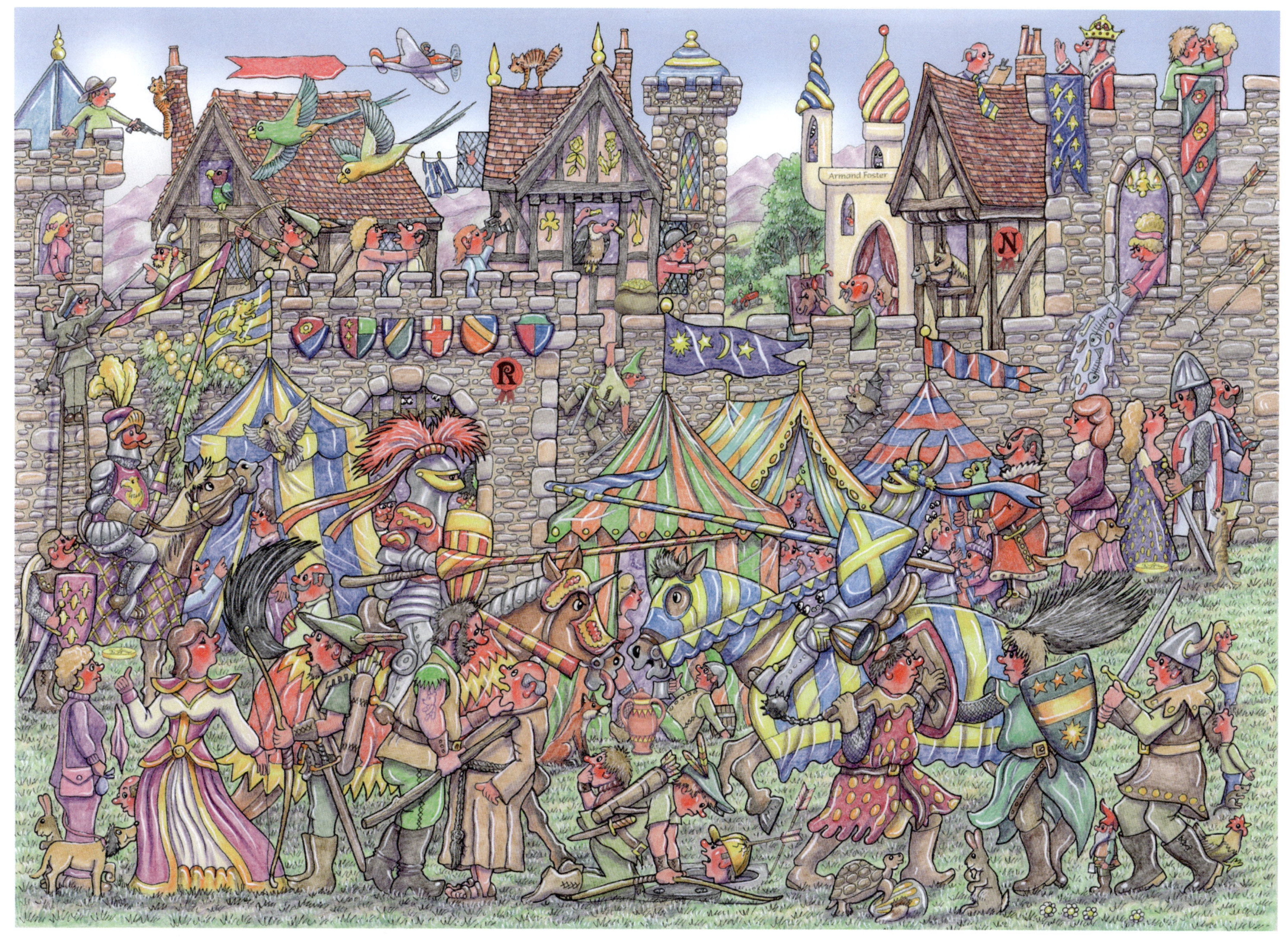

Armand Foster

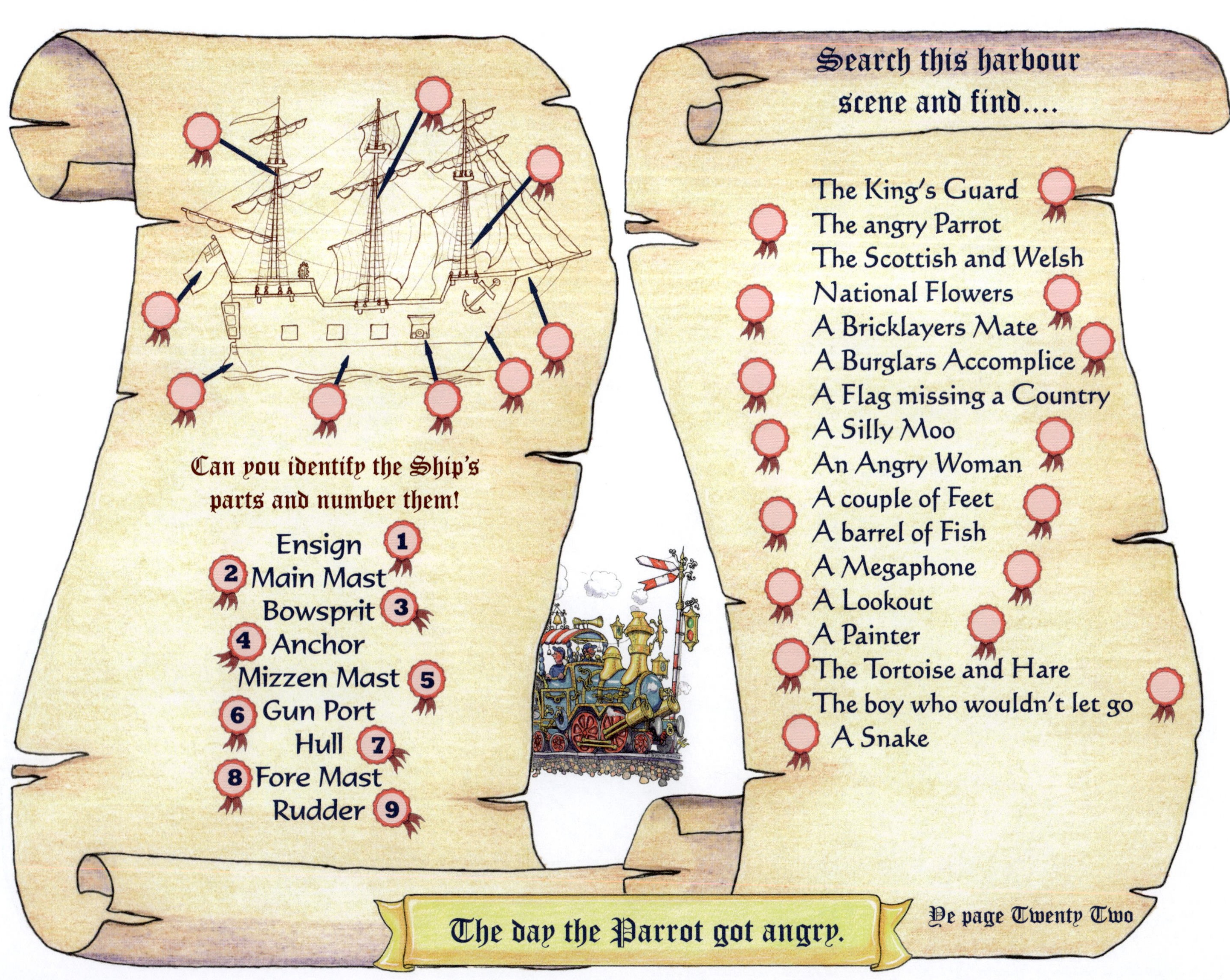

Search this harbour scene and find....

The King's Guard
The angry Parrot
The Scottish and Welsh
National Flowers
A Bricklayers Mate
A Burglars Accomplice
A Flag missing a Country
A Silly Moo
An Angry Woman
A couple of Feet
A barrel of Fish
A Megaphone
A Lookout
A Painter
The Tortoise and Hare
The boy who wouldn't let go
A Snake

Can you identify the Ship's
parts and number them!

Ensign  1
2  Main Mast
Bowsprit  3
4  Anchor
Mizzen Mast  5
6  Gun Port
Hull  7
8  Fore Mast
Rudder  9

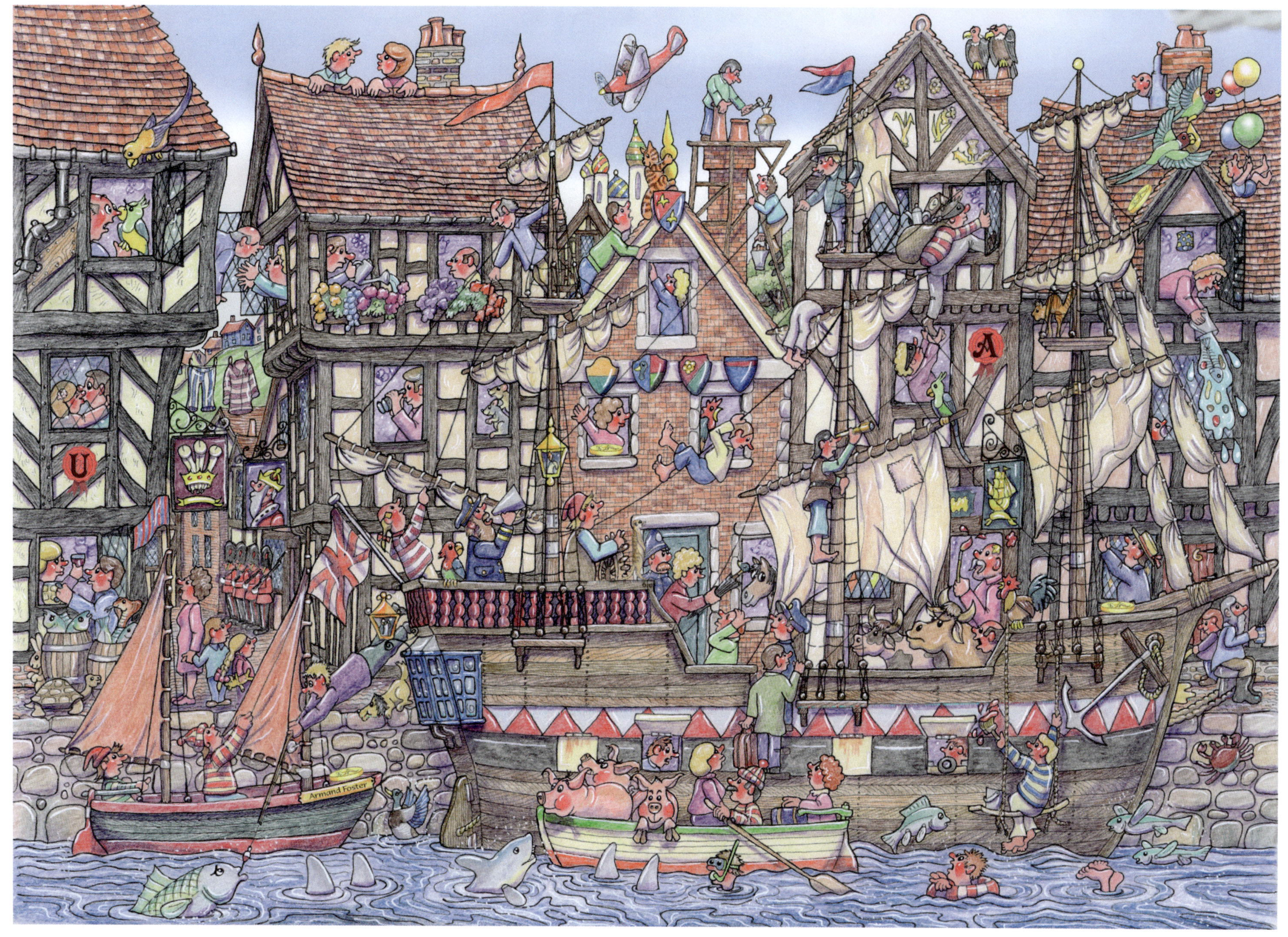


Ye page Twenty Three

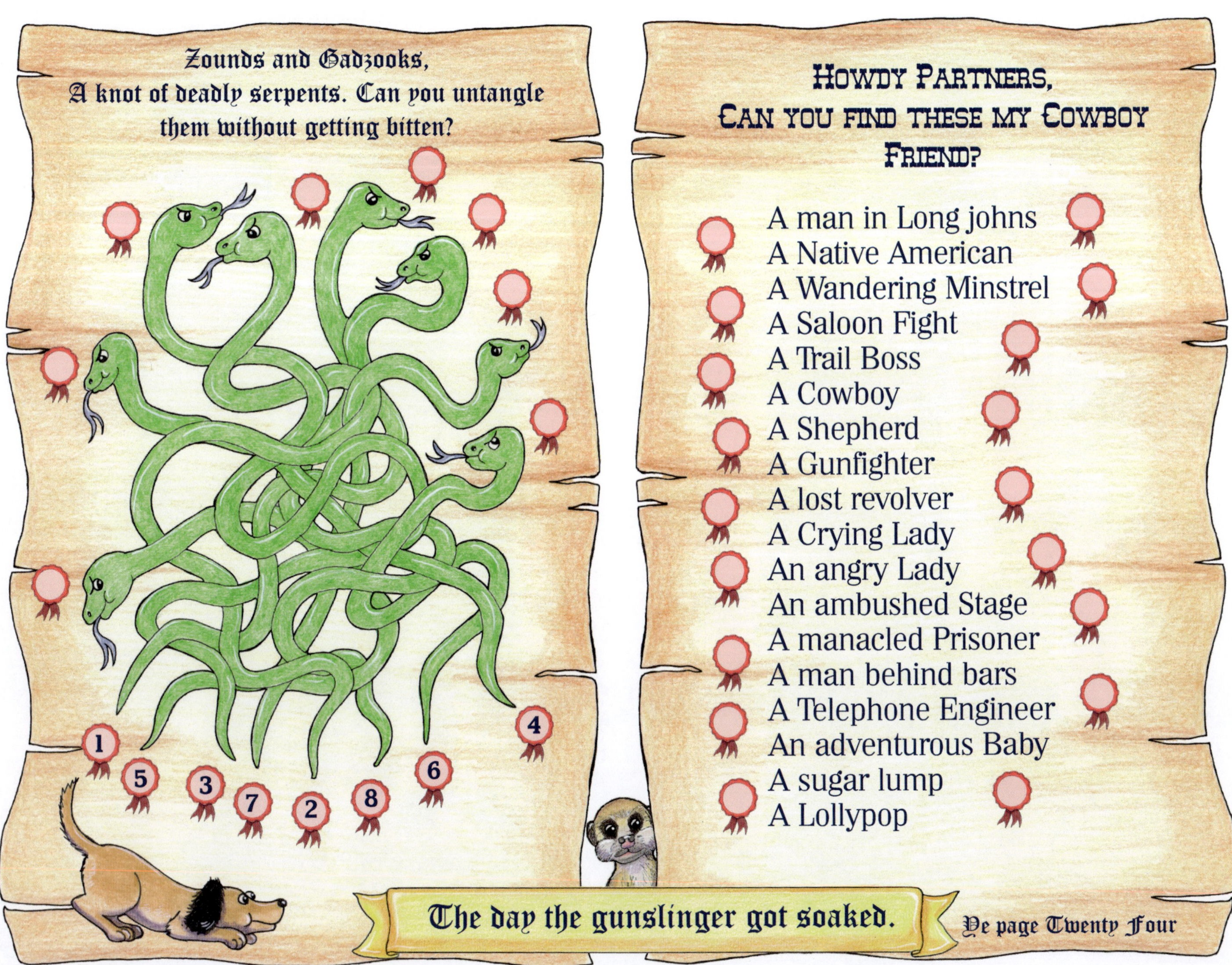

Zounds and Gadzooks,
A knot of deadly serpents. Can you untangle them without getting bitten?

1
5
3
7
2
8
6
4

HOWDY PARTNERS,
CAN YOU FIND THESE MY COWBOY FRIEND?

A man in Long johns
A Native American
A Wandering Minstrel
A Saloon Fight
A Trail Boss
A Cowboy
A Shepherd
A Gunfighter
A lost revolver
A Crying Lady
An angry Lady
An ambushed Stage
A manacled Prisoner
A man behind bars
A Telephone Engineer
An adventurous Baby
A sugar lump
A Lollypop

The day the gunslinger got soaked.

Ye page Twenty Four

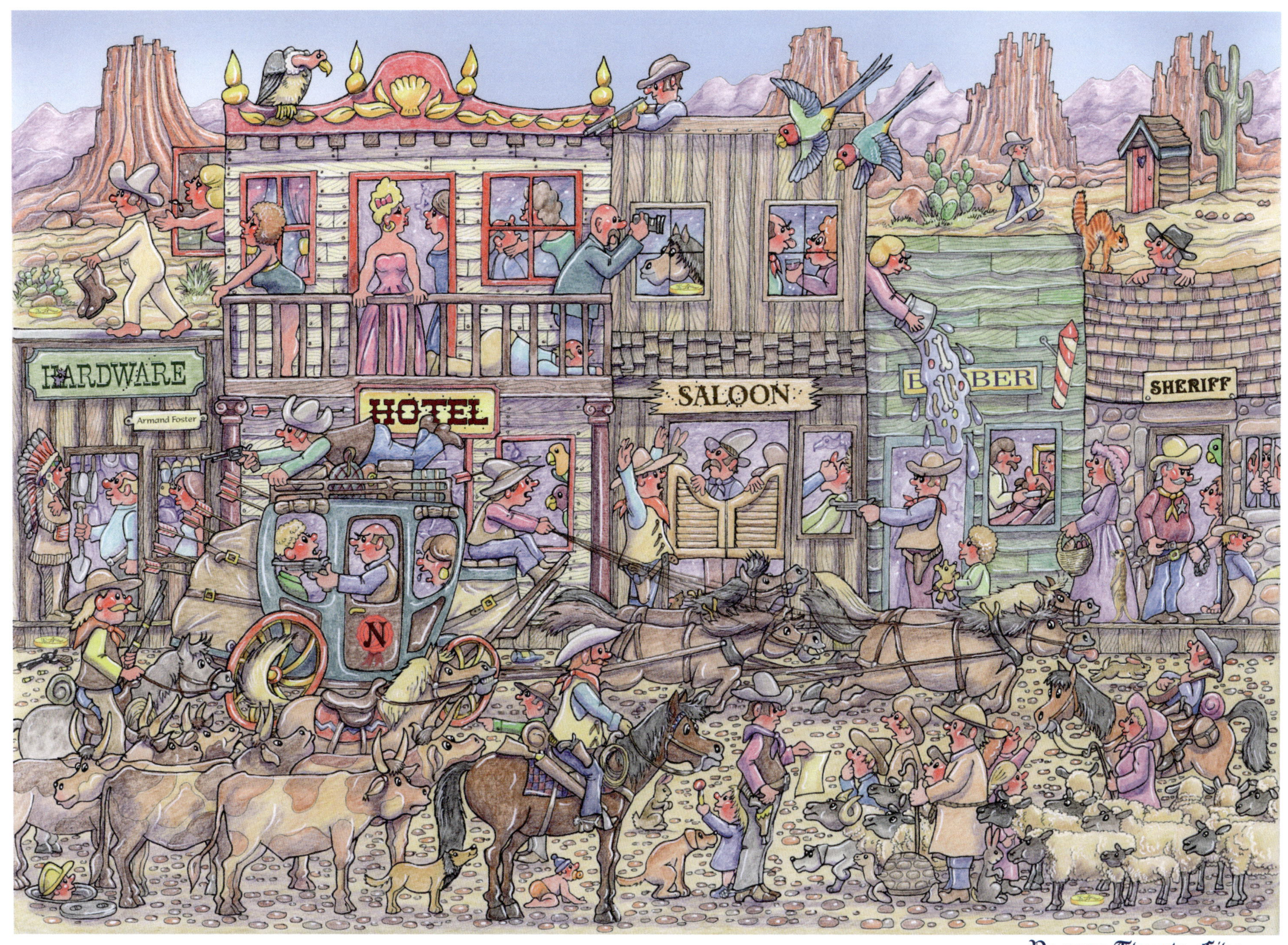

HARDWARE
Armand Foster
HOTEL
SALOON
BARBER
SHERIFF
N

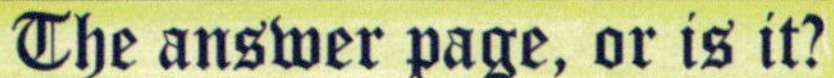

Did you find the Penguins in volume one? Well really!

The answers to the shield puzzle methinks!

Missing answers.
You tell me, what's the point of me working out puzzles then giving you the answers? What a Bounder!

Odd ones out -
Chicken, Parakeet and Pig!

The hidden word is SLEIGH

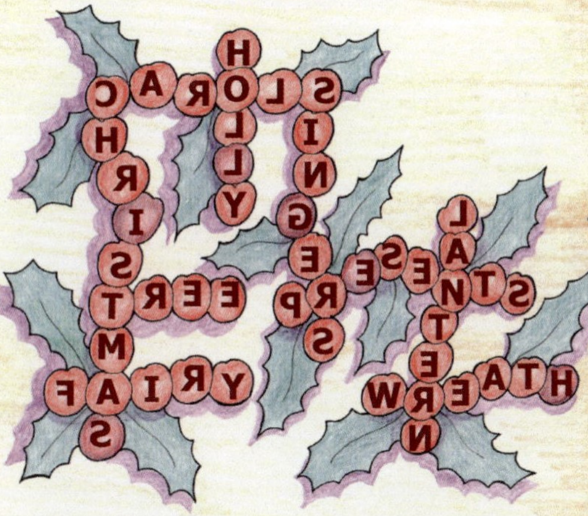

Nota bene
The thirteenth page contains treasure which is not part of the 20 differences!

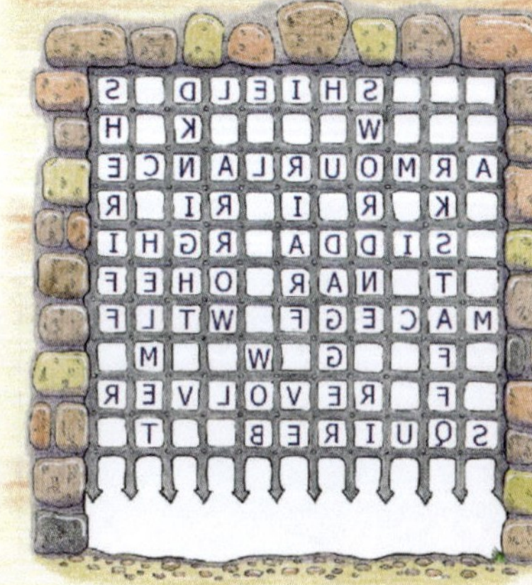

Ye Mighty Portcullis

I think there are 76 Santas but I might be wrong!

The odd ones out are an Elephant of Aardvark and of course a Marabou Stork!

There is only one Rudolf so which is the only real Santa?

Can you identify the Ship's parts and number them!

Ensign
Main Mast
Bowsprit
Anchor
Mizzen Mast
Gun Port
Hull
Fore Mast
Rudder

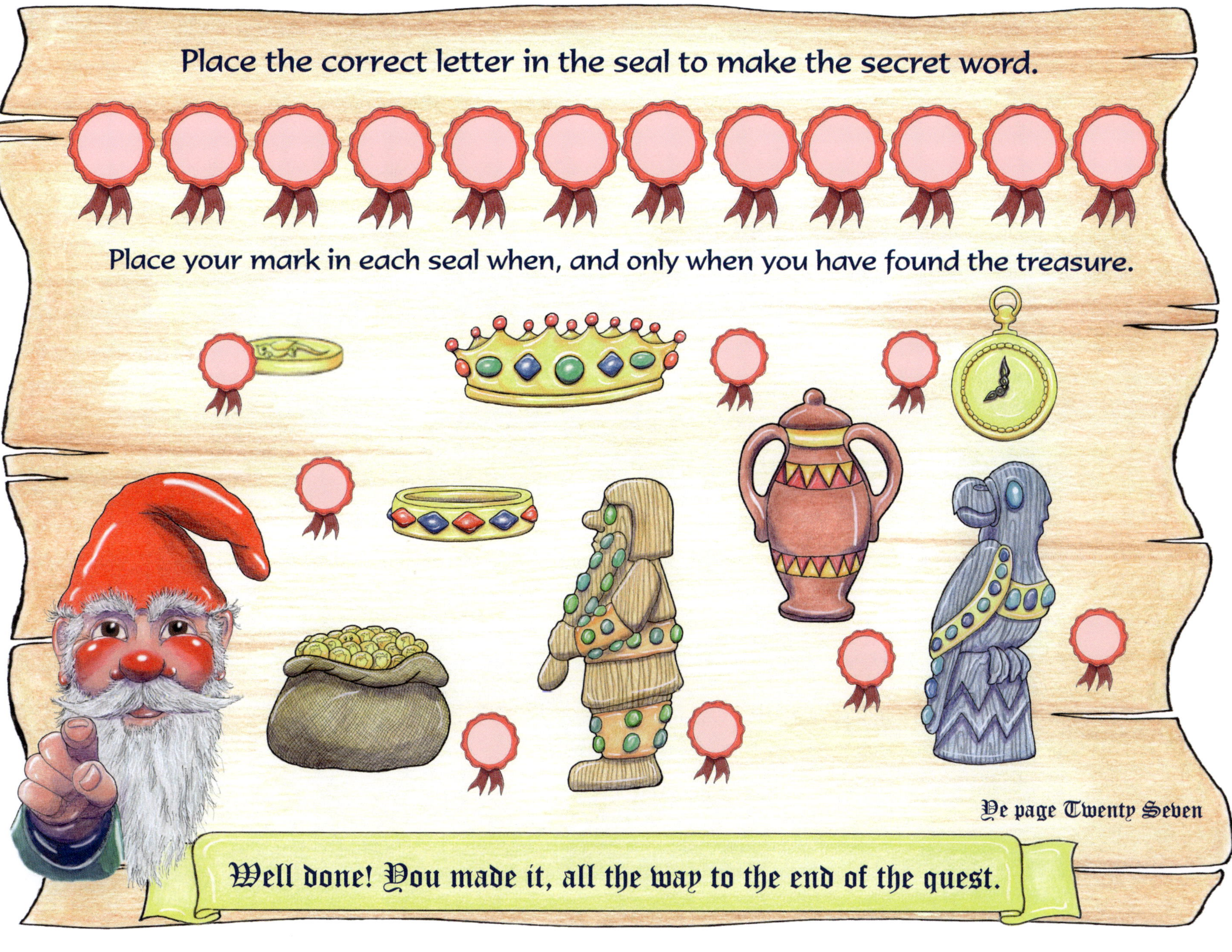

Place the correct letter in the seal to make the secret word.

Place your mark in each seal when, and only when you have found the treasure.

Ye page Twenty Seven

Well done! You made it, all the way to the end of the quest.

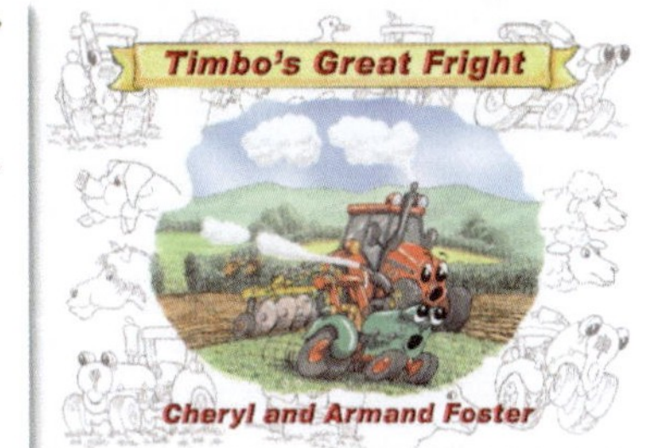


The Pigs who didn't want to go to market

Cheryl and Armand Foster



You're looking for more? gluttons for punishment aren't we?
Here's a few of his hefty tomes....

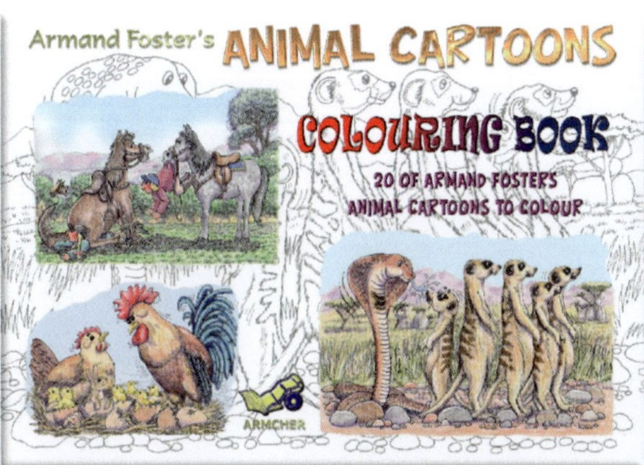


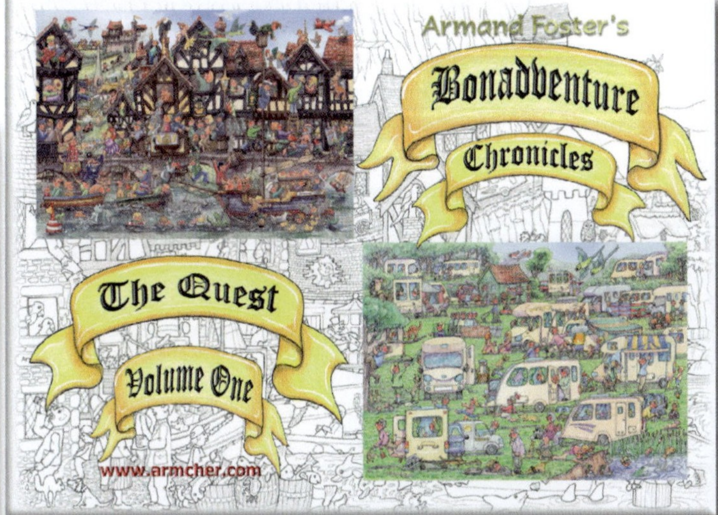


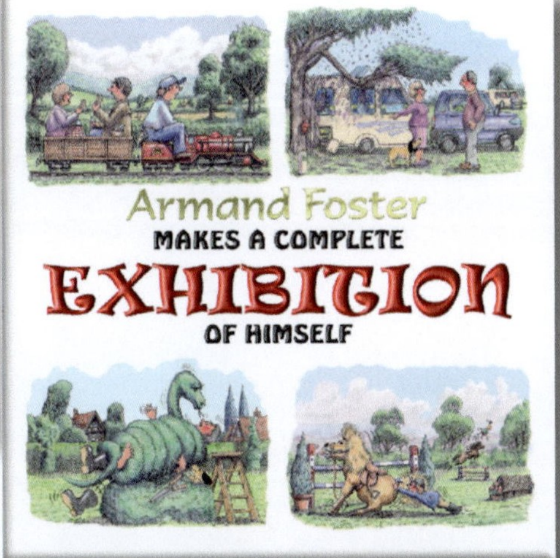


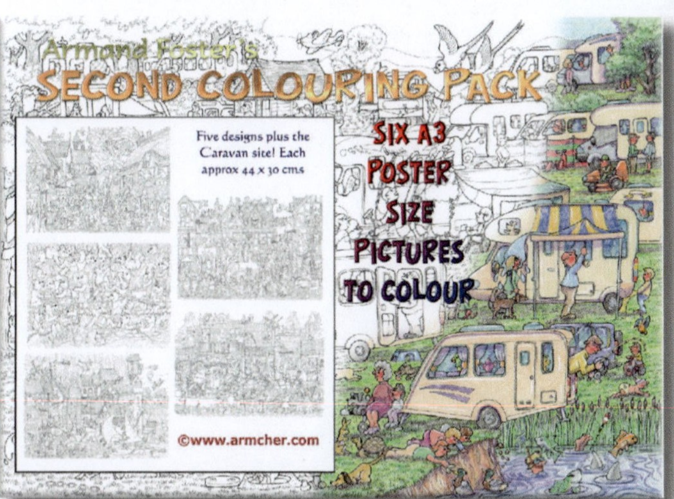


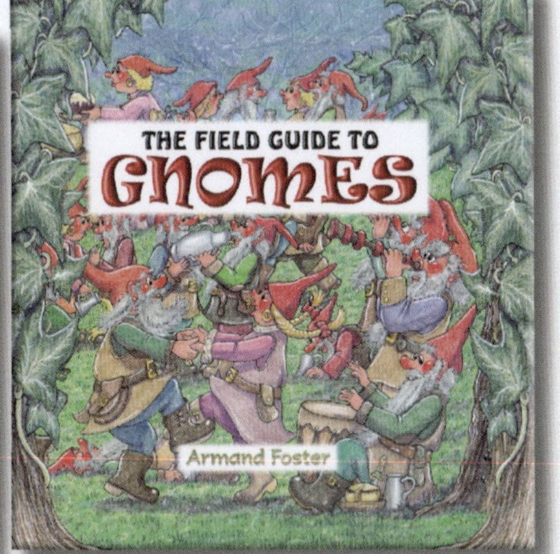


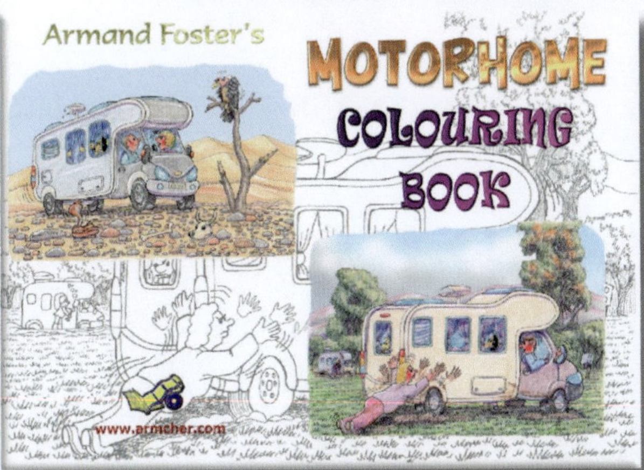

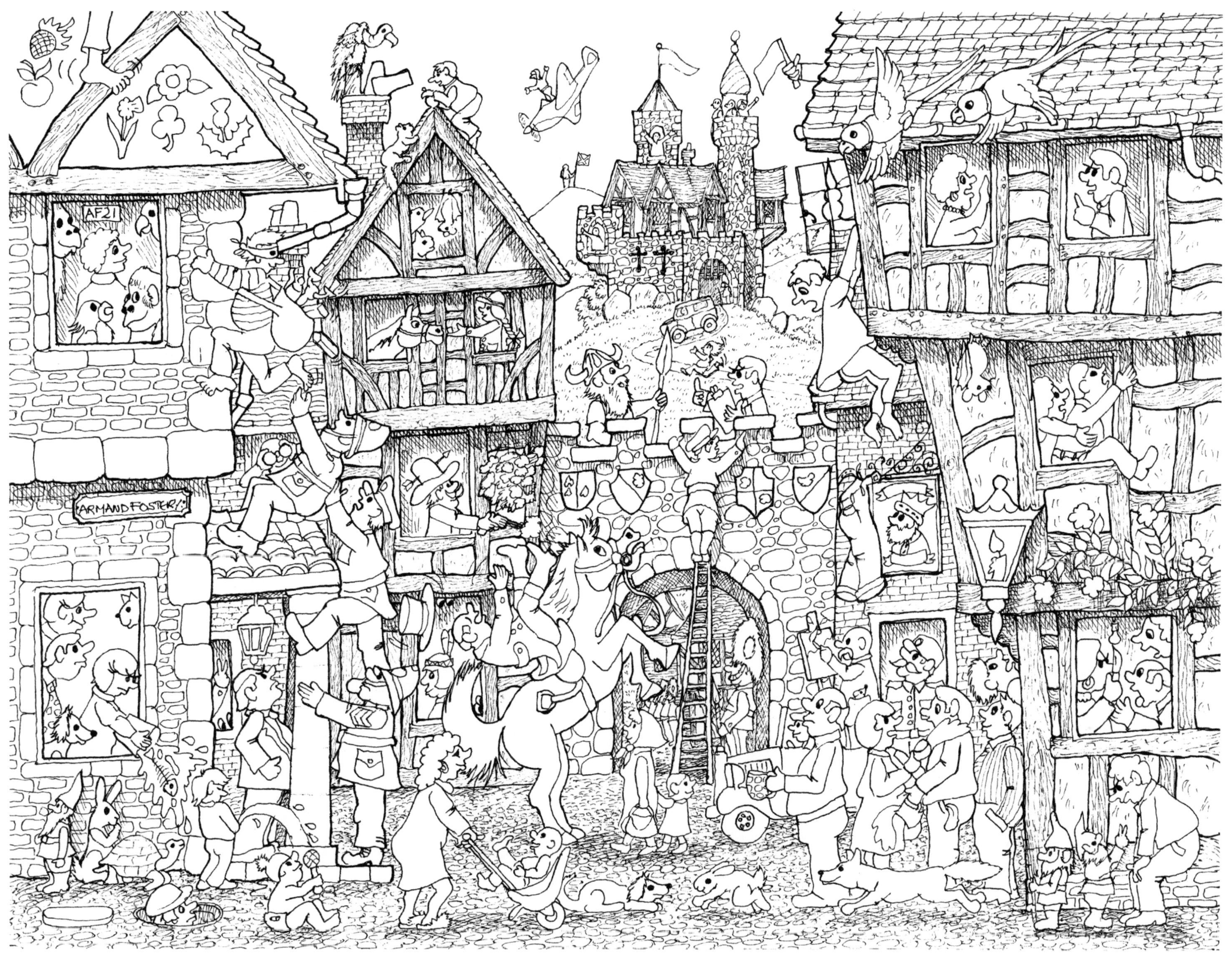

AF21
ARMAND FOSTER!!

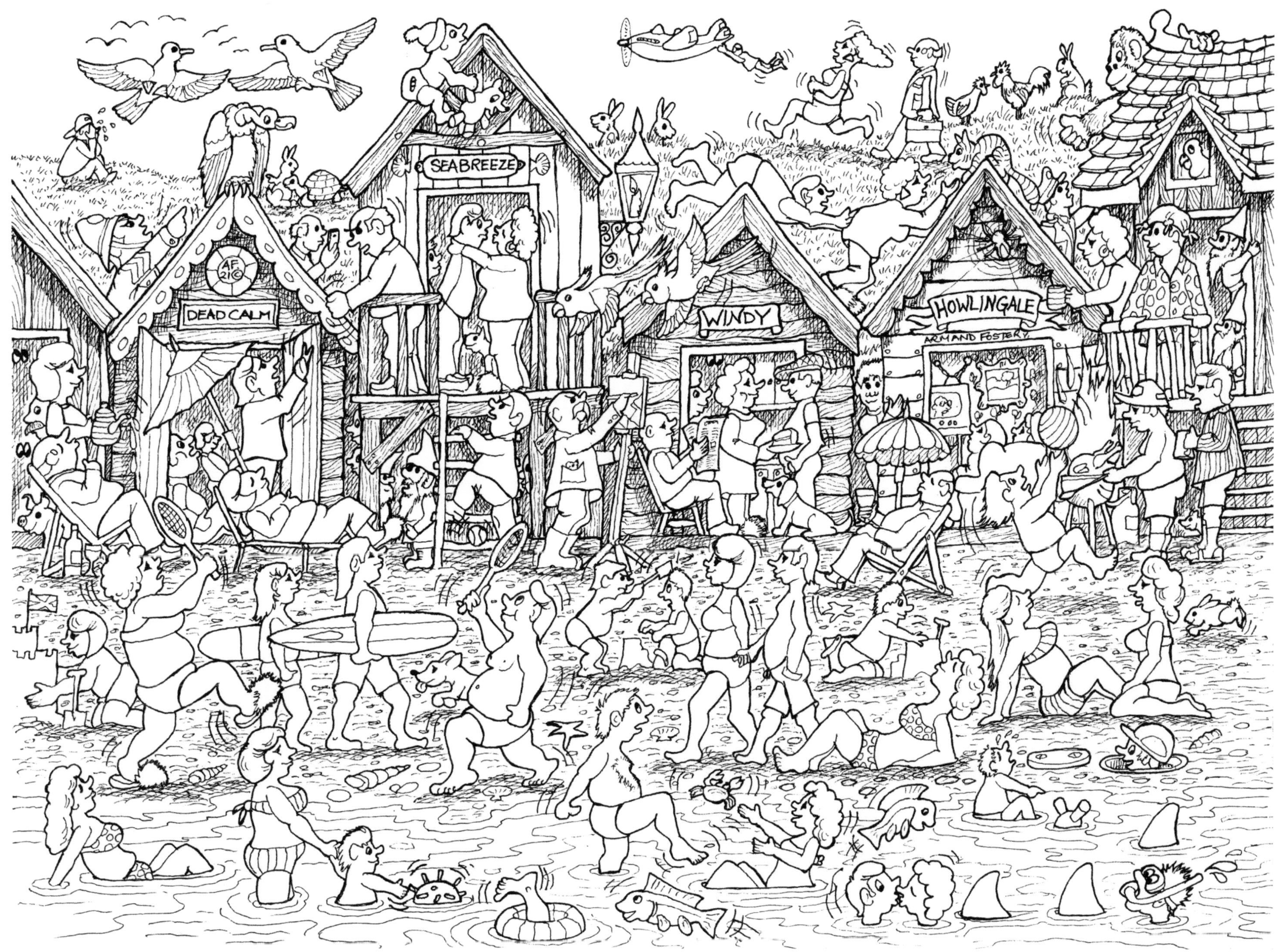
AF 216
DEAD CALM
SEABREEZE
WINDY
HOWLINGALE
ARMAND FOSTERY

Printed in Great Britain
by Amazon